Library of Congress Control Number: 2020919805
ISBN: 978-1-7359281-0-4 (Paperback)
ISBN: 978-1-7359281-1-1 (Ebook)

Names and identifying details have been omitted to protect the privacy of individuals. The information in this publication is meant to supplement, not replace, formal education or mental-health counseling.

Front cover/author images by Danni Grayson Photography
Cover design by Phoebe Brent
Consultant editing by Davina McDonald

First printing edition 2020

For permission requests, please contact publisher at:
VNW Consulting, LLC
PO Box 2255, Martinsburg, WV 25402
www.vnwconsulting.com

Contents

Underestimated

Growing in Leadership Despite
the Opinions of Self and Others

By Veronique N. Walker, Ed.D.

Contents

Contents

iii

Introduction

One day I was talking with my brother and sister-in-law, reflecting on high school graduations. I reminisced about how I attended summer school after graduating high school in order to earn a required math credit needed for college admission.

My brother responded with slight surprise in his voice, "Really?"

"Yes," I stated, "You don't remember?" He did not remember, causing me to recall that I had not told him, as he was younger and in middle school at the time, and it was not a topic of discussion later because I wanted to forget it ever happened.

Our conversation that day and my brother's surprised response, as well as other recent encounters with different people and situations, reminded me about aspects of my personal, academic, and professional journey that I had concealed. A consistent message had also been buzzing around me for several years: the power of a person's story. The message was everywhere!

Courage to Share Aspects of My Journey

When my brother and I had our conversation, I was well established in senior leadership roles. Educationally, I had acquired a doctorate and a number of other credentials. The irony was that very little of my journey had been planned. I had faced numerous rough patches that were debilitating at times and included many successes and failures all intermingled with a thread of underestimation.

Being an *extremely* private person, I knew that sharing aspects of my journey may be difficult and even embarrassing. Nevertheless, the possibility that I might embolden others by sharing my experiences far outweighed my personal discomfort.

A definition of *underestimate* is "to not realize how good, strong, determined, difficult, etc. somebody/something really is."[1] Moments of underestimation surfaced throughout my career, showing up like an unwanted house guest, whether through employers who demonstrated doubts about my abilities, colleagues who expressed their opinions about my lack of worthiness to obtain particular positions, friends who were shocked when I received certain accolades, or feelings that permeated from my beliefs.

Despite the thread of underestimation that weaved its way into certain circumstances, God elevated me to positions I and others never imagined I could attain. Prayer, support, and hard work pushed me beyond my own expectations. You see, I was born a statistic, and a series of familial dynamics experienced in childhood started me on a road of rejection that took years to traverse. Further life experiences—such as negative words spoken to and about me, actions meant to deter me, or unwise choices on my part—added to feelings of rejection, which shaped the core of who I was and played a pivotal role in how I lived my life. Other undesirable emotions such as fear, worry, and anxiety tended to bundle with rejection, resulting in a cocktail of complex thoughts storming through my mind like relentless savages.

I often chose to guard myself by hiding behind well-crafted fortified walls and iron masks, attempting to give the impression that everything was okay although I was inwardly hurting; guardedness was a defense mechanism. Others commented on how "bold, confident, and together" I was, but inwardly I quaked at the thought of being me—seemingly not having the characteristics of a leader. Although my faith has always undergirded me, life circumstances had convinced me to hide my true identity—my core likes, dislikes, talents, and beliefs—for fear of being rejected.   It was a dangerous place to be . . . a miserable way to live.

But there was hope.   The statistical implications of my formative years suggested that I would become something other than who I am today. As life progressed and I took steps to unravel the tangle of untruths wrapped around my heart, the person I was created to be began to shine. Thank God for a different outcome, the one He had designed for me.[2]

Leadership Defined

Key characteristics come to mind when I consider a leader: approachable, ethical, influential, knowledgeable, respectful, skillful, solution-focused, and supportive—to name a few. What is, however, the actual definition of a leader?

A wealth of research exists on leadership.[3] Descriptions and theories—such as classical, trait, transactional, transformational, and servant—provide insight on how leadership has been defined.[4] Words such as *power* and *authority* tend to surface when considering a leader or the belief that a leader is someone who has followers.[5] Then there is the age-old question of nature vs. nurture. . . whether leaders are born or made.[6] Simply stated, our perspectives impact how we define leadership. Considering these factors, I offer that a leader is an individual who moves others forward toward a common goal with success made evident by results.

Although learning more about leadership theories, characteristics, and styles is encouraged, the focus of this book is to provide strategies from my experiences that may be useful to you—lessons I wish I had learned prior to experiencing certain situations.

Lessons Learned

Life presented opportunities for me to grow in wisdom as I learned key insights that have supported me throughout my career, many of which were learned the hard way because I did not know whom to trust while blazing new trails. I often stumbled upon or into answers. Although others had served in similar positions before me, our responsibilities and duties differed. As the only African

American female leader and employee in several settings, my race, gender, and perceived age proved to be notable variables in navigating organizational systems. I simply wished I had known key insights when I encountered different situations, particularly as a woman of color, which is the reason for my sharing what I have learned with others . . . all in an effort to uplift someone else on her journey.

A few impactful lessons stood at the forefront of my mind as I thought about what to share with you. The title of each section represents insights gleaned from specific points on my career path and are highlighted in random order rather than the exact sequence of my career path. Most lessons were reinforced by repeated encounters in different settings. Events seared on my mind were easy to recall, while other details were taken from my journals or obtained by reviewing records from past organizations. Overall, the experiences led to an unexpected journey that illustrates how leadership grew within me despite moments of underestimation from self and others.

This book is for you whether you have felt empowered or overlooked, supported or rejected. My goal is to demonstrate that if I transcended obstacles on my career journey, becoming a well-rounded leader, then no woman is exempt from the possibility to surpass the odds stacked against her.

Insight #1: Know Thyself

While in my mental health counseling graduate program, we learned that we were only able to counsel people to the point of our own healing; it would be difficult to lead someone to a place that we had not experienced ourselves. It is, therefore, common for counselors and therapists to experience some level of personal counseling in order to work through their own issues. Likewise, it is imperative that as leaders we let down our guards, take off our masks, get real with ourselves, and explore our histories in an effort to strengthen our positive attributes and resolve anything that hinders our ability to lead.

The Heart of the Matter

What is in our hearts and minds drive how we see ourselves and function in the world, and intense moments will cause everything to rise to the surface.[7]   I did not receive formal counseling, but there were plenty of therapeutic instances that cultivated moments of clarity and healing in my life.   A main source of restoration came through my faith in and relationship with God.   There were pivotal moments of prayer, scripture reading, journaling, interactions with other believers, and circumstances which facilitated *come to Jesus* moments when I had to reconsider how I was living my life.   Working as an in-home counselor and going through a mental health counseling master's program were essential in exposing me to resources that brought to light attitudes and beliefs within

9

me. Reviewing the resources was equivalent to looking in a mirror.

As mentioned in the introduction, a sense of rejection shaped the core of my being, which resulted in a life lived through guardedness and constantly seeking validation. A common phrase used to describe me was "someone you had to get to know" in order to understand. The walls I hid behind and the iron masks I wore had been perfected to the point where very few people truly knew me. Guardedness nurtured distrust of people, ensuring that I did not let them close enough to know me. People were, with me, guilty until proven innocent and were not easily welcomed into my world.

The deep sense of rejection fueled a cocktail of negative emotions including fear, shame, doubt, and insecurity that were camouflaged by the desire to appear to *have it together*. A *sweet girl* façade combined with an *everything is under control* smokescreen was cultivated in order to become what I thought people wanted me to be. There were instances when undesirable emotions erupted through a crack in the wall or a chink in the mask, leaving me and others feeling hurt, but I quickly rebounded, making sure to patch the crack, hammer out the chink, and make the appropriate apologies. A display of emotions was unacceptable because it was, to me, a sign of weakness. Besides, what would people think? Imagine the level of frustration this way of thinking caused. In the end, not only did others not know me . . . I did not know myself.

A desperate need for acceptance ruled my life because I believed others' approval justified my worth. Striving for acceptance was my way of receiving affirmation and was detrimental because I became a people pleaser——someone who put the desires, demands, and expectations of others above my own needs and well-being. Being a people pleaser left me wide open to be manipulated by others for fear of them becoming upset or angry with me, and that led to frustration which increased my distrust of people and added to the feelings of insecurity and rejection. It was a vicious cycle——my head is spinning just thinking about it! Past hurts and disappointments taught me to keep people at a distance; years of guardedness taught me how to become the master of disguises.

A crust had unknowingly formed around my heart, leading me to unconsciously vow never to let another person close enough to hurt me again. My philosophy was that I would avoid being hurt if no one was close enough to hurt me. Imagine, if you will, a person who desperately wanted to be accepted and fit in but did not let people get too close because the relationship may result in pain. What a dilemma!

The devices I used to protect myself from others created a prison that demanded I function at high effort levels. I tirelessly worked to prove my worth only to be worn out by self-effort and disappointment, which was a form of perfectionism. Interestingly, I did not realize that I was experiencing emotional distress. Amazing, isn't it? A person will be able to function on self-will for a time, but there comes a point when the energy dies and there is nothing left to do but surrender—either to the opinions of others or a true realization of one's worth.

Examine Inner Thoughts and Beliefs

The beliefs in my heart manifested during different times along my career path. Confronting and resolving those ideas opened the door to my career and leadership development. Our education, skills, and talents may get us into a desired professional role, but the quality of our character, shaped by our beliefs, will determine if we stay in the position. We owe it to ourselves and to others to be the best versions of ourselves. This includes having the courage to examine our thoughts and beliefs to resolve internal conflicts that may hinder us regardless of the source, how long it has been present, or how painful it may be to change. Some of my self-revelations and changes occurred in the most unique situations; be open-minded and willing to embrace any opportunities to change.

For example, as an in-home counselor I was young, green, and wanted to save the world. A couple of agencies where I was employed provided trainings designed to best serve clients and to help employees maintain a temporary social work permit. The trainings focused on counseling and mental health topics such as using the Diagnostic and Statistical Manual of Mental Disorders, Fourth Edition, Text Revision (DSM-IV-TR, which has since been updated) to create effective treatment plans.

Working for the agencies brought me face-to-face with my internal traumas. Imagine sitting at a desk drafting a treatment plan for someone, reading a description of the client's diagnosis and realizing the words were describing your experiences. This happened to me several times, including once while reading the characteristics of low self-esteem. Years earlier, when confronted by a friend, I had denied that low self-esteem was a problem for me, but there was no negating the fact after reading the information. Additionally, an abundance of counseling resources was provided on how to best treat various diagnoses. Several of these counseling resources provided explicit answers to what was occurring in me and how to work through the internal conflicts. God was surely watching over my path.[8]

Has this ever happened to you? Have you ever been forced to look at yourself in the proverbial mirror and see how you appear to others? The beauty of mirrors is the opportunity to admire or adjust what is being reflected—whichever is warranted. The tragedy of mirrors is seeing oneself and not admiring nor adjusting. Such is the same in life . . . we can admire or adjust to our benefit or detriment. Acknowledging the unhealthy thoughts and beliefs I had about myself was not easy, yet I was thankful to finally have a name for my inner woes. Further clarification came through education.

Education is More Than a Credential

Education is beneficial to and often necessary for career advancement and leadership development. Certain doors will only open when one possesses a specific license, certificate, credential, or degree. However, education was for me one of the greatest tools in helping me to know myself. Whatever your educational experience has been, it is important to know that what we learn far exceeds the credential. (More about earning credentials will be explored in *Insight #3—Strengthen the Leader in You*.)

While working as an in-home counselor, I was promoted to team leader. The job required that I earn a master's degree in counseling at my own expense. Attending grad school was a pivotal season in my professional and personal life. Being exposed to more counseling theories, techniques, tools, and resources—beyond what I was learning in the agencies where I worked—further challenged me to face the emotional traumas that caused me to be guarded. Again, seeing things written in black and white gave a name to the internal emotional conflict I was experiencing at the time. I had previously prayed, "God, show me everything that is in my heart," and did He ever! Learning counseling theories, using my own personal experiences, and practicing therapy techniques shined light on the deepest recesses of my heart, bringing a more profound awareness of the scars rejection and its accompanying emotions had etched in my soul. The process of confronting negative beliefs through this mandated graduate program took years and seemed too much to bear at times.

Fear was a *constant* parasite that fueled frustration within me and consumed every ounce of confidence I had. I wanted to be content and not compare myself to others, yet I realized that I had lived my twenty-something-years—as mentioned—trying to please people and doing what they thought I should do. Even though I was doing well professionally, based on what society considered successful, I was not fulfilled and thought I was missing the mark. The simmering desire to do the unthinkable and follow my dreams was within me, but doubt in my abilities, talents, and strengths stalled me—causing every perceived wrong thing about me to haunt me in the stillest moments of the night. Thoughts of "where to go and what to do" plagued me and attempted to mute every positive thing I had learned through counseling resources as well as biblical principles.

But there was hope. Even though I struggled at times, spectacular opportunities glimmered in the light of positivity; I simply needed to change how I thought about myself because that dictated my actions. If I continued to think of myself as unworthy, incompetent, or any other negative trait, then I was going to act in those ways. If I ran around unsure of myself, then others were most likely going to be unsure of me, too. If I wanted others to have confidence in me, I first had to have confidence in myself. Be confident!

It is often said that hindsight is 20/20 and looking back I realized, as a friend regularly reminded me, that all of my yesterdays added up to today. I was not missing the mark; instead I was building a solid foundation—both professionally and personally. I needed to learn to enjoy the moment *in the moment* and to give myself a break.

Change was downright painful at times, a process in which I was often psychologically battered and bruised, but the promise of peace and clarity outweighed the discomfort of working through deep-rooted untruths. Many things overwhelmed me during grad school. However, being in a program that caused me to self-reflect—in addition to the spiritual support network in place outside of school—led me to further work through the murky waters of life, which proved to be ***crucial*** to my professional and personal growth. The developed counseling skills and earned credentials became stepping-stones to better career opportunities, while the 2½ years of grad school were among the most clarifying moments in my life. Although the agency did not pay for the master's degree, it was worth every penny.

As you are working through your education, whatever level of education that may be, take advantage of opportunities to maximize the experience far beyond the credential, for doing so may be a life-altering experience for you.

Valuing Your Identity

Our worldviews are shaped by various factors such as our race, gender, age, culture, family structure, religion/faith, geographic location, and socio-economic status. These factors impact our core beliefs, drive our decision making, and are often associated with a privilege and a stereotype. Take a moment and think about it. What is a privilege connected to age? What is a stereotype linked with gender? I encourage you to take a moment to identify privileges and stereotypes connected with each factor mentioned, and others not stated, as the factors may perpetuate bias in and towards us—biases usually reflected in our interactions with others.

Be prepared for people to judge and treat you by their view of who you are, some with the intent of holding your identity against you in any way possible. It's unavoidable, so know your rights and determine to what extent you will exercise those rights in various encounters along your career path. Most importantly, learn and love the components that shape your identity.

Our View of Others

A part of knowing our identities is knowing how we view others. We all have biases that shade our perspective, some of which are deeply engrained in the fabric of our minds to the point that we do not recognize the notions exist within us. Unpacking our prejudgments is essential in determining how we may resolve our biases and best relate to people, particularly when assuming leadership roles because we influence others with our expectations.

Others' View of Us

Knowing ourselves and valuing our identities helps us to remain grounded in light of how others view us. As an African American woman, and due to various societal factors, I am purposefully conscious of my surroundings, paying attention to who and what is around me and how others respond to my presence—and vice versa—because of my identity, especially my race and gender.

When considering my work experiences, an awareness of my race was often present, but working in the educational system made me more keenly mindful of my race, gender, and perceived age, and the impact each had on my professional role. The reality is I rarely knew which aspect of my identity was in play at any given time, and that led me to think I had to always be on point and work harder to validate my credentials.[9]

Several noteworthy experiences were gained while working as a school counselor in locations that were historically known for racial tensions. These locations were initially my least desirable options in my search for new jobs because of my preconceived notions, the unknown about how I was going to be treated, and the potential of placing myself in uncomfortable situations. The locations were, however, exceptional learning grounds where I was well respected among my employers and colleagues. Navigating the learning curve and proving myself were necessary, but I thrived and worked to serve all aspects of these organizations well, proving that sometimes the least desirable action is the best step to take.

The locations were not void of microaggressions—indirect, subtle or unintentional comments or actions based in discrimination[10]—most of which stemmed from persons who did not work in the buildings, including when outside individuals seeking the school counselor assumed a different person served in the role rather than me. This assumption was made evident when I stood in front of my office door during class changes and visitors walked right pass me to get to a different individual, assuming the other person was the school counselor. Although I was frustrated when this occurred, my view was that they were not used to seeing—or perhaps did not expect to see—an African American woman in the position of school counselor.

Other instances of microaggressions occurred when I worked with students and families. When racial incidents occurred, equitably working through situations was essential. Yet, during a requested classroom race-relations presentation, a handful of students expressed that it was unfair that they had a Black school counselor. I was the only person of color in the room—and employee for that matter—and was in shock, trying to determine if I was hearing them correctly.

The teacher stepped in and asked the students to clarify their statements. The students provided the additional rationale that I was going to be unfair and automatically side with students of color when racial incidents occurred. Half the class nodded in agreement and the other half was astounded that such had even been stated. The conversations delved deeper and the students' dialogue became more intense, with some not understanding why special considerations needed to be given to African Americans such as a month to celebrate history, a cable television station, or the opportunity for new families of color to move into their community.

I remained professional in my responses while the conversation continued, yet inwardly I was unnerved by the commentary in the room, as that was the first time I had professionally experienced such blatant efforts to preserve the status quo and their White culture, particularly in the students' community. I left the classroom and made my way back to my office to decompress.

The teacher came to my office shortly thereafter apologizing for the commentary and suggesting that I should have given them a piece of my mind. I replied, "No, then I would have confirmed their stereotypical beliefs." Sometimes we simply have to take the high road even when the low road is looking pretty good and we're ready to embrace it. The classroom conversation was necessary to expose biases and increase respect for cultural and racial differences. The experience also reminded me how my skill-level was judged based on my skin color, which was a part of my identity. When we are able to stand strong in our identities, then others will have a difficult time derailing us.

Our Views of Ourselves

Understanding our personal histories helps us better appreciate our identities, as each of us has risen above an obstacle that promised to hinder us. Pause right now and reflect on your life. Pinpoint one difficulty—no matter how large or small—that you have encountered that troubled you at the time, but you now celebrate because you weathered the storm and learned a valuable lesson. If you have yet to experience difficulty, then know that when you do encounter something, to keep moving forward because what does not destroy you only makes you stronger.

Taking the time to understand my identity—particularly the cultural, racial, and spiritual aspects—was empowering because it provided context to the sacrifices, hardships, contributions, and successes of others who came before me. More revelation occurred while I was working on my doctoral degree, further supporting the notion that education is more than a credential.

As I moved through the required courses, one leadership class set the tone for my research topic. I discovered limited information existed on women in educational leadership roles and even less information on women of color. This led me to examine perceived strategies and barriers of African American women moving into the superintendency. I researched the history of African American women in lead educational positions, from the 18th through 20th centuries. This resulted in me learning aspects about my race and gender that I did not know—particularly about the contributions of African American women to the field of education.[11]

Exploring my family history and the stories of African Americans and women overall allowed me to rest more confidently in my skin and stand on the shoulders of their achievements. It helped me understand that some of my experiences were not unique; I could learn from their examples. Taking the time to fully know, accept, and appreciate yourself (flaws and all) and every aspect of your identity will strengthen your acceptance of your worth.

Self-Preservation: Know Your Worth

Your balanced mental, physical, and spiritual well-being are essential to assure self-preservation and promote a healthy understanding of your value. When you know yourself, value your identity, and recognize your worth, you will be less likely to accept anything that diminishes you, including your own negative self-talk; we are our own worst enemies at times! The key to knowing your worth rests in building self-confidence—belief in oneself and one's abilities. Reading through various articles and books regarding women in leadership brought to light the importance of self-confidence—a critical ingredient for a woman to be effective in her role, considering there are many opportunities for a female leader to be challenged regarding every aspect of who she is.

Speaking from experience, building self-confidence stems from getting to the heart of the matter by examining internal thoughts and beliefs, replacing negative self-talk with positive affirmations, experiencing healing from past hurts and traumas, and knowing who you are based on your identity. Your awareness of self-worth will mature through supportive environments as well as trials and hardships that will teach you how to stand up for yourself. My faith in the scriptures helped strengthen me as it spoke directly to what I was experiencing; it enabled me to counter negative internal chatter with uplifting truths. Furthermore, I strove to listen to, read, and watch enriching material. Even though identifying ways to build self-confidence sounds easy, it may be painfully challenging to resolve the things that broke your confidence in the first place. Notwithstanding, building your self-confidence is worth the effort!

A benefit of knowing your worth is self-preservation which results in positive outcomes such as (a) eliminating unhealthy comparison and competition, (b) strengthening the ability to establish boundaries, and (c) cultivating mental, physical, and spiritual well-being.

Eliminate Unhealthy Comparison and Competition

Comparison and competition each have positive and negative attributes depending on the motive of the one exercising the behaviors. Have you ever been told to surround yourself with people who challenge you, uplift you, are smarter than you, or reflect your aspirations? When a woman is self-confident, she is likely to function in ways that inspire growth and yield positive results.

A time when comparison was beneficial to me occurred when I was in college and changed my major to psychology with a minor in communications. Observing other students while participating in my classes convinced me to go the extra mile in order to be marketable in the workforce. I was nowhere near the confident woman who knew her value, but it was during the season of observing other students that my work ethic intensified, producing positive and negative results.

The pros included learning the benefit of surrounding myself with people who stimulated my thoughts and prompted me to seek better opportunities, which was invaluable when I needed inspiration. The con was the tendency to strive for perfection—an illusion that fed the unproductive responses within me when imperfection occurred (which was often!)—and led to unhealthy comparison and competition.

A lack of self-confidence may fuel jealousy and fierce competition, resulting in actions such as self-defeating behaviors, needing constant attention, putting others down to make oneself feel more important, or striving to be number one at any cost—even if it means sabotaging others to get what one wants. Be aware that other elements exist that cause unhealthy comparison and competition but focusing on knowing your worth is a way to eliminate these negative actions.

As graduation neared, my resolve to be self-confident and go the extra mile crumbled. I was once again entangled in a web of doubt. I had been a student for most of my life and the prospect of moving into the unknown was terrifying, especially as I compared myself to friends who appeared to know their future plans while I was seemingly going with the flow.

Earlier I shared that I had received a promotion to team leader while I was working in a community agency. It was during this time on my career path when another moment of comparison and competition flourished. The appointment demonstrated that the supervisors saw leadership qualities in me when I had yet to fully realize the characteristics within myself. Being promoted in this close-knit organization was the first time I was responsible for supervising and evaluating other individuals.

Although my supervisors tapped into my leadership potential, a lot of growth was needed as I struggled in my new role. We team leaders were supervised and evaluated, yet no efforts were made to provide formal leadership training. Thus, I carried out my responsibilities through collaboration, trial and error, and by applying what I had learned from experiences gained in other entities. The familiar threads of underestimation and competition weaved doubt through my experiences, however, as I compared myself with two of my colleagues who had also been promoted. I felt inferior because of their popularity among staff members. My struggles may or may not have been perceived by my colleagues because, again, I had perfected the art of hiding my true feelings.

I kept working hard on the things I did well with the goal of exceeding my employer's expectations. This approach helped me to stay focused and combat unhealthy forms of comparison and competition. I'd be remiss not to state that healthy and unhealthy comparison and competition are inevitable. Others will compare you to someone else and will compete against you but avoid giving energy to any of their negative intentions, although experiencing such may lead to learning opportunities for you. Understand your worth knowing that you have nothing to prove to anyone and choose to champion others while learning from their example. Above all, simply be your best (notice I didn't say do . . . be!!).

As I moved through the career path, my self-confidence increased due to many variables, leading me to a place where I was able to authentically establish boundaries, self-advocate, and support others.

Strengthen the Ability to Establish Boundaries

Boundaries are *essential* to self-preservation. Relationships, including professional connections, benefit from boundaries—guidelines that define expectations such as acceptable behaviors and attitudes and the extent of interactions. Boundaries fluctuate as relationships evolve, causing interactions to become more relaxed or stringent depending on the nature of the changed relationship. The ability to establish and maintain boundaries correlates with how a woman views herself and others.

One example is the ability to say, "No." Let me be clear—I am not speaking about neglecting or refusing to fulfill assigned responsibilities. If, however, you are asked to perform illegal or immoral actions, or if the workload begins to impact your mental, physical, or spiritual well-being, then other steps designed to preserve your integrity and health are warranted.

If you have ever experienced seasons in which you were a people pleaser (such as I had) and have yet to fully understand your worth, then you most likely have found yourself in situations where you were manipulated by others. How do you respond to an employer who continually adds to your responsibilities without providing the resources for you to effectively fulfill your role? Do you divulge information to colleagues who want you to share news that, if they break confidence, may cause an issue between you and those about whom you are giving the information? What do you do when a group of colleagues, whose company you enjoy, become known as causing conflict and you want to distance yourself? How do you respond to the direct report who often verbally disrespects you?

The aforementioned scenarios are examples of when clear boundaries, a strong self-concept, and the willingness to resolve conflicts will most likely result in favorable outcomes towards self-preservation. I have found that as long as I was doing what people wanted me to do, they were happy with me and things were ok. But the moment I began to say, "No," or do things based on a different perspective, issues began to surface. The following are examples of techniques that I have used as resolutions to the aforementioned scenarios:

•Have a conversation with your employer about plans to help you effectively fulfill your workload, including more funding, help, or realigning duties.

•Determine if divulging the information to your colleague will be helpful or harmful, taking into consideration their trustworthiness and your responsibility to maintain confidentiality.

•Decide if aligning yourself with various colleagues is the reputation that you want for yourself, because we tend to be judged by the company we keep.

•Meet with the direct report to determine the root-cause of the unfavorable actions, working to resolve the tensions and using the organization's corrective measures, if warranted.

The key is to address boundary issues because what is not resolved only festers. Your mental, physical, and spiritual well-being are worth the effort.

Cultivate Mental, Physical, and Spiritual Well-Being

There's an element of knowing our worth that relates to self-advocation for the sake of protecting our mental, physical, and spiritual well-being. One way to self-advocate is to say "No," especially when stress and anxiety threaten to disrupt our health and peace of mind. This lesson, however, was learned the hard way.

I was working for an organization, at one point in my career, where my duties skyrocketed. I endeavored to prove myself and used my job performance as self-validation. Seeking worth through achievement was a dangerous trend because my duties steadily increased yet my work often went unnoticed and unsupported. Thoughts of job effectiveness frequently massaged my subconsciousness, as I steadily became a jack of all trades and master of none; I wondered if a difference was truly being made.

As time progressed, a mostly manageable workload became taxing, as duties were slowly added each year and I was eventually assigned to lead copious programs, supervise upwards of 85 individuals, and manage more than 100 phone, email, in-person, and letter contacts per week with various stakeholders and with little to no help. Although administrative assistance was nearby, I—for several reasons—ended up completing most of the assignments by myself. That may seem appropriate, but most people in my role, in other organizations, had some level of consistent assistance. Yes, I accepted help when such was offered and available, and deeply appreciated when a new colleague was added to the team who helped immensely, but I was often on my own. I later realized that others in the organization experienced similar scenarios.

Detailing my responsibilities will not fully capture the complexities of functioning within the role, which included learning to work with various personalities, procedures, and deep-rooted office "politricks" (a term used by member of my local community) all with the goal of operating in the best interest of the organization's mission and vision. Long, late, and weekend hours were plentiful, and the stress level was daunting. I had responsibilities outside of work duties as well, so most evenings were full of activities. When there were evenings or weekends where nothing was scheduled, I savored those days and enjoyed the solitude of my home, fiercely protecting my time. I had little patience when I thought someone was disrespecting or wasting my time.

It wasn't long before my health was impacted, resulting in accumulating doctor visits and medical bills. I was doing too much and not taking care of myself. A change was in order.

I began to self-advocate about the extent of my work duties and eventually submitted a proposal to my employer about my role in the organization; others who recognized the load also advocated on my behalf. I had been an unnoticed workhorse yet advocating for myself—and being self-confident enough to do so—resulted in a positive transition in my overall mental, physical, and spiritual health. I discovered the significance of stress-management, which I needed to facilitate by making significant changes. It's up to you to determine what is best in your situation.

Insight #2: Most Experiences Have Value

Take a moment to think about someone you consider to be successful (however you define success), a person about whom you may find yourself thinking, "I want to be able to do what he or she does." Chances are whomever you identified reached their level of success by taking a series of small steps that consisted of much sacrifice. Yes, some people are afforded opportunities that quickly open doors for them without much effort. Everyone else, however, tends to start in a place other than the most important leadership position.

As we move through life, we acquire competencies valuable to our future endeavors, regardless of how minute the experiences that led to the skills may seem. It was only when revisiting my past that I recognized seemingly insignificant events as pivotal moments that served as cornerstones to competencies used throughout my career. One such occurrence was in high school when my school counselor told me that I was not college material.

The counselor, during my senior meetings, may have surmised my college ability by looking at my average grades and standardized test scores, and by reviewing the fact that I had failed two math classes and was, as a result, missing a math credit to enroll into college. The opinion may have been formed by hearing me answer "No" and "I don't know" to questions such as "Where do you want to go to college? What do you want to do? Have you applied to any schools? Have you taken the ACT . . . SAT? How will you pay for school?" Regardless of the rationale, the counselor's words stung.

Failure is a Stepping-Stone to Success

Have you ever thought about what you would tell a younger version of yourself? I have, especially as I reminisced about the rough patches I encountered, including my high school situation. The counselor's words were hurtful, but the responsibility about my future belonged to me. Thankfully, other people encouraged me, including my Mother who most certainly told me where I was going to college—an affordable, local option. Positive parental guidance and support are essential to the success of any child and my Mother provided that to me.

College was in my post-secondary education plans in high school and I was on the path to obtain the required college entrance courses. Yet failing a math class meant I had enough credits to graduate high school but needed a math course to enter college. As a result, I was sitting in a summer school class at my alma mater a few days after graduating. The tenacity I showed to earn the required credit was the trait of perseverance—or persistence—being cultivated within me.

Perseverance became the hallmark of my journey because my life was destined for many more of life's small inconveniences and failures. Although God had a wonderful plan for me, the road was not always easy to follow and was affected by numerous variables, including my decisions. I would now tell my younger self to stay calm when I stumbled and fell, regardless of how many times that occurred, and to boldly get up and keep pressing forward because all of the failures were mere stepping-stones to a beautiful destination.[12] What would you tell a younger you?

Building the Leadership Foundation

Although I did not realize at the time, seeds for a few of my knowledge, skills, and abilities (KSA) were planted when I was in college. Life took on a more meaningful purpose during my first semester. I planned to make better grades by studying and becoming a powerful businesswoman, a goal which contradicted the shy, introverted person that I was. Average grades in high school led to provisional college enrollment and remedial courses my first semester. I expended substantial study effort and the hard work paid off, resulting in one of the best semesters I had in college.

While in college, I became involved in different activities, including a multicultural program designed to develop leaders of color. Since my high school grade point average was low, I did not qualify to be a part of the college's multicultural leadership program. I was, however, actively involved in an ancillary group that provided a space of belonging for students of color. Exposure to both groups planted in me a seed of activism that evolved into my profession. Thus, although I was not a standout student, nor one appointed to leadership because I did not demonstrate such at the time, my experience was not wasted. It was a platform being built to prepare me for the future. As my time in the group proves, it is good not to discount ourselves or our experiences. So, to you who may be reading this from the shadows of your life, come out of the darkness and let the light shine on and from within you.

As the semesters progressed, I became more socially involved rather than focused on classes. The poor study habits and apathetic attitude I had demonstrated in high school returned, causing me to fail several courses and experience academic probation. The counselor's words were ringing true. A change was needed, particularly since my Mother was not fond of paying for failed classes. I recommitted to succeed in college and changed my habits in order to alter my direction. Undergirded by perseverance, I: (a) reevaluated and adjusted accordingly, (b) assumed responsibility, and (c) identified positive supports. These steps helped me correct my course and further develop leadership skills.

Reevaluate and Adjust

One change involved switching my major from business to psychology and my minor was changed to communications. The new interests seemingly went against the grain of who I was because both fields involved interacting with people and I preferred to be guarded and alone. Although I wanted to focus on the writing aspect of communications, several courses required creating audio and video recordings, as well as public speaking which mortified me. The result was often a shaky voice and trembling hands whenever I had to stand and speak in front of a group of people.

Yet the very things that were uncomfortable for me (interacting with people) or frightened me (public speaking) later became a few of my strongest assets. The courses also gave me knowledge that helped me better understand myself. One such course introduced me to the Myers-Briggs personality test, which first shed light on introversion as a real and okay personality trait. Don't give up on yourself by letting the circumstances that cause you to fear today keep you from taking action because on the other side of fear is your destiny.

Once my major and minor were adjusted, I employed focus and study habits that led to academic improvement; the human service field proved to be my niche! Little did I know that the decision to change my major placed me on an unimaginable career trajectory. Each decision was pivotal in contributing to who I am today and is the reason making wise choices is essential.

Assume Responsibility

Another change that occurred in college was when I began paying my own tuition. This motivated me to do better because I did not want to waste *my* money. I began working part-time jobs more consistently, striving to navigate the school/life/work balance, and further developing the strong work ethic that I desired to exhibit. Now I must admit, there were times in college when I was not interested in working and a more relaxed approach was taken. Notwithstanding, most employers, in my experience, recognize hard workers and tend to reward such. The outcomes of hard work for me, however, depended on the organization. Some companies rewarded my efforts with awards and promotions, while other companies took advantage of my work ethic by adding copious *other duties as assigned.* Thus, the skill of self-advocation became a necessary tool because I had to either learn to speak up for myself or be manipulated. These experiences affirmed for me that our development and success is largely our responsibility.

Identify Positive Support

People along the way supported me and helped me to progress. As a young woman who had yet to develop the capacity to believe in myself, those who offered words of affirmation proved to be the extra boost I needed to keep going.

While in college, being rooted in faith was the most essential asset in my efforts toward academic improvement. Each woman has something in life that contributes to her mental, physical, and spiritual well-being. For me, it was my relationship with God and connecting to Him through prayer, listening to, playing and singing gospel/worship music, studying the Bible and meditating, and attending various church events—all of which counteracted the negative self-talk occurring within me.

These activities inspired me to reach for the best in life. It was, in fact, in the Church where several of my leadership skills were cultivated through various activities, which I later found through research was similar to other African American female leaders.[13] Leadership skills can be cultivated in any setting if we keep ourselves open to the possibilities.

My latter years in college proved to be the strongest academic period of my college experience and the competencies stayed with me. The high school counselor's words proved to be wrong . . . I simply needed to mature, find my interests, and surround myself with people who had my best interest at heart, which helped me to get me through many challenging days.

Failure was not the end of the story but was instead a launching pad into my future. Sometimes giving ourselves space and time to figure things out makes all the difference in the world, but keep in mind that there is no need to always *figure things out* by yourself. Whom do you have in your corner?

That Old Familiar Feeling . . .

Worry fueled indecisiveness about my future as graduation neared. This doubt led to uncertainty about what I wanted to do in the field of psychology. A visit to my academic advisor initially appeared promising. The advisor suggested I pursue my aspirations in the field of psychology through human resources rather than clinical psychology—diagnosing and working with individuals one-on-one. The advisor's intentions were unclear, but the words stimulated that old familiar feeling of underestimation. I perceived the advisor was telling me, "You will not be successful practicing clinical psychology," even though I received strong reviews from my clinical internship experience and was praised for being one of the best students they had at the time.

I followed the advisor's suggestion. I graduated college with a degree in psychology and a minor in communications but decided to pursue the business route again, aiming toward a position in the human resources department of an organization.

Insight #3: Strengthen the Leader within You

Leadership occurs in many contexts such as in a family home, a volunteer community group, a faith-based entity, an educational system, or a Fortune 500 company—to name a few. Chances are you have served in a leadership capacity, have been encouraged to assume a leadership role, or have been a role model to someone who wanted to follow your example. Taking time to strengthen the leader within you is essential to maximizing your effectiveness in any role that you assume and involves several strategies including (a) accepting that you *are* a leader, (b) confidently assuming the leadership role, and (c) pursuing formal education, licensure, and credentialing.

Accept that You are a Leader

I, at times, was tapped for leadership roles long before I felt like a leader. People saw leadership in me before I saw it in myself. One instance occurred while I was working at a call center. The orientation process included training which explained the criteria for the role as well as the timeframe projected to reach specific benchmarks—several months for new employees. I achieved the goal within the first month. That was a time when my introverted way of providing short, blunt answers came in handy; since I limited small talk, my calls were focused, businesslike, and resolved quickly.

Our metrics were shared during various team meetings, and I often received accolades from my supervisor and a few team members. Due to consistent improvement in meeting company metrics, I was tapped sometime later to become a member of a team of helpers, which was an entry-level leadership position, who guided other call operators when they had questions or when a customer requested a supervisor. I doubted myself and tried to rationalize why I was selected to be a part of the team of helpers even though the recognition was the result of my work ethic. What are you letting stop you from being the best leader you were appointed to be?

Another profound moment occurred when I received a promotion in the community agencies previously discussed in *Insight #1: Know Thyself*. Sometimes people will not like you because of the potential they see in you but thank God for those who are selfless enough to uplift you to greatness. If an employer sees characteristics in you that he or she wants to use to move the organization's vision forward, then you will be promoted over individuals who have served the company longer or are seemingly more experienced than you. Accept the recognition, even in the face of tension that may result, *and* strive to be someone who lifts up others!

The challenges I encountered early on my career path manifested my Achilles' heel experienced throughout my professional journey: exuding confidence, appropriately articulating my point of view, trusting my instincts, knowing when to let situations naturally resolve, and building credibility. Yet accepting my responsibilities and functioning to the best of my ability—even when afraid and unsure—was what strengthened my internal resolve and eventually sharpened my skills. Now let me be clear, growing in leadership was a process. It took years of triumphs and failures for me to become seasoned; I continue to learn to this very day! It was, however, when I began to accept myself as a leader that I began to improve in leaps and bounds. What will it take for you to accept that you are a leader?

Confidently Assume the Leadership Role

The most poignant change in my leadership occurred later in my career. An unexpected blow occurred when I received a promotion after serving three years in an organization. Someone I thought was supportive of me led a charge of slander against me, and a season of scrutiny from others ensued. Once again, I was reminded that promotions were bittersweet when the joy of career advancement was juxtaposed with the sadness of being torn down by perceived allies—a topic further highlighted in ***Insight #5: The Power of a Support Network***. God had certainly strengthened me because there was a point in the past when the negative campaign had the potential to devastate me—a time when I lessened myself to keep the peace because I could not handle the scrutiny nor the rejection.

Not this time. I was determined to be myself and no longer shrink from the woman God had created me to be, refusing to allow insecurity and fear to rob me of my destiny. I finally understood, after past experiences, that people were going to have something to say regardless of what I did. Please know that no matter what you do, someone is going to be displeased. Lead anyway! Yes, you will make mistakes just as you will have great successes. Accept your mistakes, celebrate the successes regardless of how large or small, and take time to maximize your strengths and acknowledge your weaknesses.

Maximize Strengths and Acknowledge Weaknesses

We all have strengths and weaknesses. Let's own our strengths and confidently function in our strong points! Owning our weaknesses is equally important because trying to deny weaknesses is unproductive. One of my strengths also happened to be a weakness . . . attention to detail. Now what, you may be wondering, is the weakness in wanting to complete things well? The devil is in the details, it is said, and it was my attention to such that caused me to hinge on perfectionism, resulting in internal pressure and unrealistic expectations. It was intolerable!

Fortunately, one of my career experiences freed me from the tyranny of perfectionism. I had begun to regularly make errors to the point where I daily exclaimed, "That's my mistake for the day," some minor, others not so minor. Making errors and learning from the mistakes enabled me to produce quality work without the added stress.

Have you ever had a strength that first appeared to be a weakness? Or perhaps it *was* a weakness that changed due to skill building, practice, and repetition? Whatever the case, I can relate. Recently a colleague complimented me on my public speaking skills, exuding accolades about my voice tone and ability to engage the audience. I thanked my colleague while chuckling to myself, amused because my colleague did not know the horror that used to grip me in the past when public speaking; it was a true weakness.

Approximately mid-way through my career journey, my public speaking skills had drastically improved from my college days but speaking in front of an auditorium full of stakeholders, sometimes hundreds of people, caused me to shut down; I simply refused to present. My boss never forced me to present and instead communicated the information on my behalf. This occurred the entire time that I was employed at that location, and I was thankful for my employer's understanding.

As I moved to a new work location and realized public speaking was required, I determined to leave the debilitating fear behind when initially faced with presenting to a large audience. Although nervous, I walked to the microphone and gave my presentation. My new colleagues complimented me, not knowing that talking in front of a large group represented a victory for me. Transcending the hurdle of fear was empowering and was achieved through prayer, preparation, and practice.[14] It took years and much repetition for me to become skillful at speaking in front of people. Nervousness still skims the edges of my thoughts when I have to present, but I press forward.

Maximizing strengths and acknowledging weaknesses is where knowing thyself is helpful. Invest in learning your personality, skill set, leadership style, and characteristics through available assessment tools (see Appendix A). Focus on building your strengths rather than dwelling solely on your weaknesses. On the other hand, be sure that a perceived weakness isn't simply a strength needing time and attention to be developed. The beauty of being a leader—or a team player in general—is that we do not have to know how to do everything! Instead, identify and draw on the strengths of others to make for a dynamic team experience.

Find Balance in Tooting Your Own Horn

As a person who was used to working in the background, who rarely announced what I was doing, and had become proficient at streamlining processes, it appeared to some in several organizations that I was doing nothing. People often said they did not know what I did. Initially I toiled to justify myself and to help them understand my duties, but I soon concluded that they were only able to understand if they walked in my shoes. Isn't that true of everything? We can fully understand someone's situation only when we walk a mile in their shoes. I simply got tired of using energy to validate my worth—although that was a double-edged sword since there was no other way for others to hear about what I was doing if I kept silent.

Later in my career journey I made the decision to create a document that outlined what I had accomplished. I started a database that consisted of all the trainings, workshops, non-degree graduate courses, and summer programs that I had facilitated, co-facilitated, and organized while I worked in a certain organization. I stood amazed at how much I had completed because, at that point, there were over 100 items in conjunction with my other job responsibilities. As a result of this exercise I can affirm that it's a good practice to document progress as a visual reminder of the work you've done.

When the idea to create the database first surfaced, I was unaware that it would later become a defense tool used to affirm the work that had been done during my tenure. Additionally, I had often felt overlooked and under-appreciated, and thus surmised that the work I had completed was done in vain. There were times when I sat at my desk organizing trainings, while thinking about the uselessness of it all. Yet through a series of connections, other entities began contacting me to put together trainings for their organizations. I was able to use the material completed over the years—the work I felt had been done in vain. This reminded me to not lose heart in the work that I was doing.

A supervisor once told me it was important that I share with others what I was doing, as great things were going unnoticed. I initially found the advice challenging to do, but soon learned that it was possible in an authentic way. Tooting our own horns takes balance in that it is important to receive credit and recognition for our work without appearing to be a braggart. Depending on your industry, newsletters, blogs, or simple social media posts may be the tool to help you demonstrate the work you do.

Another practice I used was to ensure people received credit for their work, utilizing opportunities to publicly thank and congratulate them. This helped to build trust, respect, and social capital with colleagues and direct reports. Their responses affirmed that most people welcome appreciation.

Finally, I have learned to graciously accept when others give me earned accolades for a job well done *and* to say thank you to others for their support and jobs well done. As a leader, and a human being overall, show gratitude; most people are more willing to work with others who do not take them for granted.

Your Leadership Will Be Challenged

Leaders represent a plethora of things to others. Therefore, being in leadership may make you a target for both positive and negative attention. As the leader in a particular organization, I did my best to represent the company well, and doing so sometimes drew positive and negative attention. People approached me at times in ways that mirrored their feelings about the organization. I generally separated myself from negative projections when such occurred, understanding that they were not attacking me personally but instead were attacking the organization where I worked.

However, there were situations in which people's projections were pointed and personal; they used sharp words intending to be hurtful. Their words and actions indeed stung, and I had to navigate how to handle my responses. Simply pausing worked wonders, allowing me to calm down and give the most helpful resolution to the conflict, which sometimes involved not responding at all.

Supervising others was also a testing ground for my leadership skills. The complexities of navigating numerous personalities, agendas, motives, and varying levels of skills, all while dancing across the learning curve was rewardingly challenging.

I strived to respect others and their expertise and had a lot of success doing so, while other times I stumbled due to mishaps. As my confidence grew, however, I began to have *defining moments* with people. I was either going to continue to allow myself to be addressed in certain ways or establish the authority assigned to me. This was a balancing act that involved triumphs and trip-ups.

Once I supervised an individual whose years of experience almost matched my age. Several clashes and tough interactions occurred but one small gesture on my part finally broke the tension and set us on a path of trust which allowed us to accomplish great things together. It simply took time. This interaction reminded me to be willing to be the peacemaker for the common good—as much as possible—even when all the effort in the world might not be reciprocated. Several instances involved my direct reports having more years of experience than me. I was careful to show respect for their years of service without downplaying my leadership. If you are ever faced with a similar circumstance, remain confident in your skill to lead because you were chosen for a reason.

As I progressed as a leader, respect for me noticeably grew with some individuals once they believed I had their best interest at heart. Then there were others who longed for the day when I would be replaced. You simply cannot make everyone happy! All in all, I worked hard to ensure those I led had what was needed to operate effectively in their positions, all with the goal to demonstrate appreciation for their hard work.

Pursue Formal Education, Licensure, and Credentialing

This insight may seem to be in stark contrast to the previous message about education being more than a credential. However, for the purposes of this example, formal education, licensure, and credentialing are necessary steps to become best prepared for your current position and future career endeavors. Education may be acquired through various forms including certifications, licensures, participating in workshops or webinars, taking classes, or seeking degrees; the options are extensive. The key is to determine what criteria is required to become knowledgeable and skillful for the goal you want to achieve.

I pursued further study in most cases after being promoted to a new position. A degree, licensure, or credential undertaken was either a job requirement or pursued for asset building to assure readiness for future opportunities.

Earning a master's degree in counseling was necessary to maintain my leadership role in the community agency. My colleagues and I worked full-time while attending a class every Thursday evening after work for 2½ years, with a few make-up classes on weekends. We drove 1 hour and 45 minutes to attend a four-hour class before returning home and reporting to work the next day. The work/school/life balance was taxing, but we adapted to our routine.

A professional license was required to clinically counsel clients and is what I was on course to do. I therefore began planning the process of becoming a licensed professional counselor (LPC) which, at the time, required 2400 hours of clinical counseling work, one hour of face-to-face supervision for every 20 hours of clinical work, and passing the National Counselors Exam (NCE). My job at the time was in a clinical counseling setting, allowing all of my job responsibilities to be counted toward my licensure. Once I finished my master's degree, I was going to be on track to become an LPC within a couple of years after graduating.

I made a career switch to school counseling during the last semester of my master's degree program. This required that I take an additional five courses, including an internship and a Praxis (qualifying) exam in order to become a certified school counselor. Completing the courses and earning the required certifications took an additional 1½ years beyond earning my masters.

I decided to continue pursuing the LPC licensure, which took longer to complete (a total of five years) because only a small percentage of my school counseling work was usable toward clinical hours. A case load of students was created each school year, with parent and caregiver permission, to provide therapeutic services in an academic setting in order to meet the clinical requirements. It was an arduous process, but one that I deemed necessary.

The purpose of sharing my educational path is to demonstrate, as an example, the level of sacrifice that may be required for you to accomplish your goal, which may be more or less than what I have shared depending on your desired outcome. Notwithstanding, my experiences have empowered me to boldly encourage you not to grow weary in working hard, because in the end the tasks will bear fruit if you do not give up, often times when you least expect it.[15]

An additional move I made later on my career path while working in the educational field quickly demonstrated that if I desired professional growth, then a different skillset and other credentials were needed. Through guidance and deep reflection, I opted to enroll in a doctoral program while dually earning administration and supervision certification after my first year of being in the newly acquired position. I also began to attend as many trainings as possible to stay abreast of trends in my areas of responsibilities. I surmised that doing otherwise may result in my becoming professionally stagnant.

Sacrifices were necessary in order to grow professionally and sharpen my leadership skills, regardless of the inconveniences—and there were many! The beauty of acquiring education is that no one can take it from us, and it will—most likely—open different doors. Stop with the excuses, if that is your present stance! Make the necessary sacrifices to gain the education and credentialing you may need to make your dreams become a reality.

Insight #4: Risk-Taking is a Game Changer

Risk-taking comes with unknowns such as whether the change will be worth the effort and if we are prepared for what stands on the other side of our decision. Once, while working in a community agency, I decided to apply for a managerial position which put me in direct competition with a colleague who ended up being chosen for the role.

The hiring manager later told me that although I was not selected, my performance in the interview was surprisingly strong. I interpreted the manager's response as underestimation. Although my self-confidence had improved, the sting of rejection left me feeling like a failure. Yet in the end, when one door closed, another one opened. Shortly after this incident, I landed a new role outside of the organization, one that I had desired as well. Taking the new role was risky because I was only guaranteed a position for a year. Nevertheless, I moved ahead and had no regrets because the employment term was expanded for as long as I wanted to be in the role.

Let my story encourage you to keep an open mind when a door closes, because the timing may not be right for a particular opportunity or, perhaps, something better is in store.

Become Uncomfortable with Being Comfortable

The problem with dwelling on the past is that it may rob us of our future and can keep us from moving toward a brighter tomorrow. Exchanging negative self-talk with self-affirming truths is a strategy to strengthen the leader within you.

Discontentment—which stemmed from my desire to be more challenged and expand my learning opportunities, to recreate myself, or to relocate to an organization that was more appreciative of the work I produced on their behalf—proved to be a factor in most of my career changes. Unfortunately, in one instance early in my career, I did not realize the extent to which I was discontented until a phone call changed the trajectory of my career path. *My* rude response to a caller was the last straw for me; it was time to go. This is where my first clear-cut career change was made because of my harmful attitude. How does an unhelpful attitude ever serve anyone well? It doesn't!

Job changes may be required to preserve one's sanity or that of others, particularly if the job is bearing on one's peace of mind and satisfaction, or if it is causing stagnation. There were instances when the decision to adjust my career path might have appeared impulsive to onlookers, but the steps were well-reasoned actions that changed my life, further defining my career path. What brighter tomorrow is waiting for you to make a change today?

Expect the Unexpected

Was there ever a time when an unanticipated opportunity was presented to you in an unexpected package, and the opportunity resulted in the best option for you? That has happened to me several times and the experiences cultivated competencies I used later in my profession.

Six years into my educational career, which was still early in my overall career, a desire for professional growth led me to consider an entry-level position within an educational organization that piqued my interest. Initially doubting my abilities, I decided to forego the opportunity but was later encouraged to apply, which I did close to the last day of the opening. Sometime after, I was contacted for an interview and was later offered the job, which I accepted.

Being hired into the position caused me to stand amazed at what God had allowed me to achieve. I reflected on the significant impact of my decisions, whether large or small, for even the seemingly small decisions were life altering including the decision to apply for the role. I was almost afraid to be happy because staying grounded was of utmost importance to me. Experience had taught me that it was better to stay low, or humble, than to be brought low, or be humbled.

What I was about to learn was that the blessings of God may also bring many challenges and responsibilities, for there was another side to being hired. Instead of starting the new job as a joyous moment in my life, it ushered in one of the toughest seasons of my professional career. Experiencing unforeseen hardship in the position snatched the proverbial rug from under me and stripped away the confidence I had gained. A cocktail of familiar negative emotions consumed me, with fear being the boss. The experiences knocked the wind out of me and brought me to my knees for several reasons.

Almost immediately, several individuals with whom I had built friendships over the years changed. They either spoke against my ability to facilitate the role, against the necessity of the role, or by exhibiting envy. People I did not know expressed similar qualms regarding the job, partially because I was unknown to many in the organization.

Having the wind knocked out of me solidified the lesson I've learned about not working to please people. I discovered that when I kept quiet and to myself—or even if I didn't—people made assumptions, invented stories, questioned motives, and spread falsities. What kept me going was a core group of family and friends who upheld me and became a source of strength for me during one of my lowest points professionally. What could have destroyed me only made me stronger in the end. As a result, I challenge you to stay true to yourself and keep moving forward regardless of what may be said about you or the amount of support you receive.

The Reality about Small Beginnings

My experiences being in the background, not receiving attention, and working through those feelings prepared me for my entry-level educational role, as much of the work initially garnered little recognition or support from key individuals. I had to get used to motivating myself, as well as rely on my trusted support system.

The beauty of being in the role was that I was given a blank slate to cultivate the position into what I envisioned it to be. I began working feverishly to build rapport with stakeholders in the organization by visiting them, attending meetings, and establishing a network of individuals who were likeminded in moving toward systemic change. I researched, read many policies, figured out ways to promote the programs I directed, supported my colleagues' programs, presented information, deepened my technological skills, attended trainings and workshops, and sought assistance from individuals in other organizations who did similar work.

Key life lessons taught me to not despise small beginnings.[16]   I developed the mindset to focus on facilitating quality opportunities rather than attracting numbers. The first training that I developed and organized had 12 participants from a pool of more than 2500 employees. As time progressed and the quality of trainings spread by word-of-mouth, people began to register for trainings so that waiting lists were eventually needed. My hard work and effort began to speak for itself. I learned to welcome and celebrate any successes—whether two people showed up or the venue was packed—and I encourage you to do the same.

There will be Growing Pains

Every organization has a culture; learning organizational culture and knowing how to navigate it is crucial to your success as a leader. Culture shock overtook me during my transition into a mid-level career position. Webster's dictionary defines culture shock as *a sense of confusion and uncertainty sometimes with feelings of anxiety that may affect people exposed to an alien culture or environment without adequate preparation.*[17] The new environment was different, and I did not experience the camaraderie I had enjoyed while working in other entities. As the only African American female, I experienced tensions which appeared to stem from my race, gender, and perceived age. Even so, I was rarely ever sure which factor was being mismanaged.

I did not know the ropes of the organization such as budgeting, the politics and unspoken rules, the culture and deep connections—nor was there anyone to show me directly. I felt as though I was on the outside looking in, often stepping onto landmines and falling into pits, learning about breaking an unwritten rule because of a cold shoulder, silent treatment, or simmering tension. Yet the trip-ups helped cultivate the wisdom I needed to navigate the system, and it was wisdom that taught me to slow down, listen, read, observe, and learn what was happening.

Too many times we may throw ourselves into situations without having the right information, only to trip ourselves up . . . having enough information to be dangerous yet not enough to not look foolish and unknowledgeable. Knowing who and what we are dealing with is priceless, and by using wisdom I began to learn the organization—knowing when to speak and when to be quiet, when to push an issue or when to wait, who to ask for help, and how to help others.

I also quickly learned that how I operated in previous roles to build social capital was not going to be effective in this organization. As a result, working in integrity, establishing reliability, being authentically me, and keeping my name out of drama became my goals. It was important to be a woman of my word and to execute my duties in the highest quality because I wanted my name to be associated with excellence.

Insight #5: The Power of a Support System

Trust was essential to the health of my role as a leader because working with others was the only way to professionally thrive and build needed programs.[18] I built trust with others the same way I learned to trust——through confidentiality, integrity, authenticity, and respect.

From Isolation to Connectedness

A coworker in one organization once courageously said, "We don't know anything about you. For all we know you walk off the face of the earth when you leave here." I smiled and walked away more determined to be an enigma. I initially believed that developing friendships with coworkers was unwise and maintained strictly professional rapport, which had both positive and negative results—— positive in establishing professional boundaries and avoiding most office drama, and negative in not being able to build professional networks and get to know others and vice-versa. This belief and practice later changed.

You will most likely spend a significant part of your day with your colleagues. Being closed to building professional relationships with others may result in isolation, misunderstandings, job dissatisfaction, and competition, whereas having an in-house support system tends to be helpful in making the work environment more enjoyable for everyone. Taking the initiative to talk to others may be the very step needed to move you from isolation to connectedness.

It is important to use wisdom when determining with whom to align yourself because there are those who may not have your best interest at heart and others who may hinder your professional growth because of their reputations.

What if, however, you *are* alone and isolated in your organization and do not appear to have anyone to mentor or sponsor you? Then look to build collaboration with people outside of your company, whether through professional affiliations, community groups, spiritual advisors, or personal support networks. Once when I was working in a role few people before me had executed, an individual in a nearby organization who served in a similar role became a mentor to me and assisted me in numerous initiatives. Her mentoring was priceless. I had to be willing to ask for help, as will you if you find yourself alone.

Securing Allies and Deflecting Naysayers

Identifying people within an organization who were allies—persons who demonstrated a willingness to be a support system—became a priority as I progressed on my career path. Leadership misjudgments occurred in a few instances because of the persons on whom I relied for support. Other times I formed professional connections with people in different organizations, as they too felt isolated at times. My goal was to identify individuals who kept information confidential as I did the same for them. Through this approach I became part of a network of people from diverse organizations with the singular goal of supporting each other.

It is important to understand there were also those who were non-supportive. Why mention them? Because every journey has antagonists, people who *want* to see you fail and will attempt to intentionally attack your character and sabotage your work; it takes fortitude to keep going despite the negativity of others.

For *every* promotion I received, regardless of the extent of the promotion or the organization where the advancement occurred, there were individuals who offered congratulations, well-wishes, and assistance; and then there were those who were jealous, backstabbing, and contentious. There is a saying to get your expectations in line with reality in order to reduce the likelihood of experiencing frustration. My expectation rests in knowing that human beings will have positive and negative responses and reactions to the success of others. No one can escape this experience; get ready!

Ironically, I found allies and naysayers where I least expected. Unknown supporters emerged from the shadows surprising me with their encouragement, while I was deeply disappointed when someone I thought was for me ended up speaking or acting against me. As Maya Angelou stated, "When people show you who they are, believe them the first time." In other words, know your circle, or *tribe*, because there just may be a Jesus and a Judas among them, and they most likely have given you a glimpse into who they truly are. Watch their actions and listen carefully to their words because their true identity will eventually show. Regardless of what others may do, I strive to be an ally to those who depend on me for support and keep moving forward despite those who try to place stumbling blocks in my way.

Most importantly, I learned to encourage myself regardless of people's praise or the lack thereof; this took years to cultivate. Whenever I was recognized for doing well, I tended to downplay the reward or deflect the attention. In a sense, I apologized to others for doing well because it appeared to make them feel better about themselves. Gradually, this habit changed; it had to change, as my confidence strengthened. I learned not to ever hide my light to make others feel better about themselves because their opinion about me is none of my business. To you I say, "Let your light shine!"

Be Willing to Learn from Anyone

Each point on my career path had individuals who knew more than me. I enjoyed learning and was an intellectual sponge, absorbing as much knowledge as possible. Learning from colleagues who had been in the field longer was helpful, as they had mastered how to work efficiently within the scope of our responsibilities. Had I been caught up in my title and education status in various roles, I would have missed the opportunity to learn from individuals whose life experiences and on-the-job training exceeded my knowledge, skills, and abilities. Sometimes the information we need the most will be in the hands of someone we least expect. This is why it is important to respect what everyone brings to the table.

When I first entered the public-school setting, the second person in command was an expert in using the statewide software platform that contained all of the organizational operating programs, including the student database system. He provided me with one-on-one, in-depth training that I later learned was beyond what other school counselors in different schools received. The in-depth training provided technical skills that I used during my entire educational career. Thank God for those who love to share knowledge and are not intimidated by individuals who strive to soak up every ounce of wisdom available to them. I strive to be a sharer. . . .let's all be sharers![19]

If I wanted the answer to something job related, then I asked a lot of questions at the risk of being a nuisance. How else was I supposed to learn? Asking questions within appropriate contexts and observing others resulted in me learning much about organizational dynamics surrounding politics, assigned titles versus power and influence, and building social capital. I asked many questions and learned as much as possible from whomever was willing to provide information—regardless of their role. People were mentoring me even when they did not realize they were. If, as a leader, you want to know how to accomplish a task, simply ask questions.

Insight #6: Persevere

Perseverance is one my favorite character traits that has been etched into the fibers of my soul. Perseverance tends to be produced through adversity. We experience obstacles and trials that ultimately lead us to a place of maturity and completeness if we allow ourselves to be molded by hard lessons.[20] Perseverance has been the intrinsic motivator that has kept me going when I wanted to quit.

When things went well, I celebrated with the goal of staying grounded while proudly acknowledging accomplishments. On the other hand, when negativity around me was intense, I strived to nurture the trait of perseverance by focusing on positive thoughts and turning inwardly for inspiration.[21] When more encouragement was needed—which initially was often—I contacted trusted allies who talked me through the chaos.

One of my personal journal entries contained a quote from an uncited pamphlet that stated to "...surround yourself with people who believe in you, who expect the best from you, and who will even go the extra mile to see you successful" and I have done my best to follow these words. My desire to build quality programs, a solid reputation, and to drown out the naysayers further solidified for me the need to go the extra mile. Whatever you do on your leadership journey, be sure to pack perseverance in your toolkit because it will help sustain you in times of difficulty.

PoliTRICKS and Power Plays

As people move into positions of authority, their acquired power has an interesting impact on them and tends to change—or expose—their character. . .for better or for worse. *Every* organization has a culture that is governed by *politricks* (as stated by a person in my local community) and power plays.

Politricks describe politics that occur when individuals use power, authority, or manipulation to gain an advantage over someone else. . .often to achieve their mission at the expense of others.[22] Politricks in this section refers to organizational politics.

Power plays—or wielding authority to demonstrate who is in charge in order to gain the upper hand[23]—is a tool people use in politricks. Being successful in competitive environments requires knowing how to play the game while keeping your integrity intact and avoiding getting caught-up in power dynamics. This was a hard lesson for me to learn!

Politricks and power plays that I have encountered during my career include individuals who openly or secretly attempted to sabotage my work by spreading false information and using their power to shut things down. Other dynamics I faced in various organizations concerned gender roles, where men occupied most of the top-level positions, which reflected national and global trends.

Several reality checks occurred at different career junctures in my life. One check point involved a leader's expressed disinterest in me fulfilling a key element of my job responsibilities, which resulted in my perception of working in vain. The leader's stated view reflected, from my standpoint, the general opinion of others about my role and experience in the organization.

Another check point occurred when I had been working several weekends, on behalf of the organization, and requested a comp day, to which the response was, "No one told you to do that." It caused me to again wonder why I was working so hard if no one appeared to care. This incident was the first time I began to evaluate my tendency to over-exert myself for a company that did not reciprocate. I discovered first-hand that there is a thin line between loyalty and being a doormat . . . a very thin line.

As much power as I *thought* I possessed in one role, a casual meeting with an executive and a veteran employee revealed that I was simply a pawn in the organization's chess game. Although I was in a leadership position, I was not in charge and thus had another reality check. There's a saying that blood is thicker than water, and in an organization where there were long-term connections, their history together was similar to family ties which overruled any title or vestiges of authority. Unless the new employee gained the respect of the group, it was an arduous task to navigate these deep-seated connections. Yet the sweet tune of perseverance welled-up within me, and I remembered the overarching reason I was serving in the role. As a result, I encourage you remain committed to your purpose, for it will help you transcend odds.

Don't Take It Personally, Even If It Is

A key to being successful when politricks and power plays were in effect was to avoid taking things personally, even if something was meant to be personal; learning this was a long process for me. One of my roles required me to create programs with limited help or administrative support, which became the rule rather than the exception.

Developing programs created a sense of ownership for me. Instances occurred when people offered feedback and criticism, which I was sometimes hesitant to accept because of the amount of work I put into a project. . .and there were times when people's comments were noticeably personal. Yet in the end I learned to be more open to critique because I was able to use the feedback for the betterment of the programs.

I also grasped the value of pausing before responding, regardless of how long the pause may be, in order to ensure a professional response rather than a personal one, particularly when people's comments were personal towards me. How do you respond to criticism?

Be Willing to Stand Alone

As my career flourished, I stood my ground, even when I had to stand alone. There were instances in which individuals wanted me to run programs a certain way. I knew that to be effective, a delicate balancing act was needed to facilitate the programs in the way that maximized effectiveness. I also stood my ground when advocating for initiatives within the organization, such as updating and working through organizational policies to bring the initiatives to fruition. Whenever I reacted wrongly because I was offended, I had to tell myself to rise above it—no matter how long it took to do so.

A few ways I moved beyond the offense included waiting for the right timing to reintroduce the initiative, seeking guidance from a colleague or supervisor to identify how to repackage the initiative, collaborating with other individuals and departments who had common goals or more influence, or letting go of the plan.

Know and Use Your Rights

Knowledge is power and a way to be best prepared as a leader is to know your rights, particularly federal, state, and local laws as well as policies and codes that govern an organization. I have spoken to individuals who were afraid to execute the processes necessary to tackle perceived or actual infractions. I, too, have been in similar situations. Yet, as I have grown and learned how systems operate, I understand that everyone deserves to work in a safe and welcoming environment free from bullying and intimidation. Thus, stand up for your rights and the rights of others, when such is warranted.

Insight #7: Be an Example to Others

As mentioned in *Insight #1: Know Thyself,* working on my doctorate sent me on an unexpected journey of reflection that empowered me because of what I learned and synthesized with my own experiences. I read a substantial number of journal articles, books, and other research materials that spoke directly to my leadership experiences and validated the things I was experiencing at the time but was unable to define—such as power structures, race and gender roles, invisibleness, hidden and unspoken rules, having to work harder, and much more.[24] Learning about similar experiences of other women across numerous fields—both nationally and globally—showed me that I was not alone but instead a part of a community of women.[25]

It was no coincidence that dissecting the experiences of others led me to revisit aspects of my journey. My disgruntled attitude began to shift to one of gratitude as I realized that the hard work and rough times molded me in ways I never imagined were possible. Diverse work situations further exposed my strengths and weaknesses, as I was presented with opportunities to showcase my abilities and grow professionally and personally, while accepting my weaknesses. The introverted people pleaser who questioned her worth became, by the grace of God, a strong woman willing to stand for what was right for the youth and families I served.

81

The historical approach to examining the subject of African American women in educational leadership positions fueled a deep desire within me to share my story as an example to others who may have experienced or will encounter similar situations. Again, it's what I wish I had received when moving through my career path.

My journey has been shared to encourage someone to persevere—to keep moving forward. You may feel isolated, intimidated, or like giving-up along life's way. Yes—your journey is different from mine, the obstacles you face perhaps more daunting, and the critics you encounter more relentless . . . yet keep moving forward.

Even as I write this, there are dreams yet to be realized and career goals to be met in my life that are waiting on me to take a step. In fact, writing this book is the first in a series of steps that I am taking because I have challenged myself to be willing to leave my comfort zone to experience the miraculous!

What about you? Are you ready to step deeper into your destiny, whatever your aspirations may be—whether it is to become a better leader, business owner, employee, volunteer, parent, friend, or spouse? If so, then do not let the underestimation of others, or your own thoughts and past failures, keep you in a place of complacency or defeat. Our new tomorrow is waiting for a change in mindset and behavior today!

There's More to the Story

This book represents only the beginning of a lifetime worth of insights Veronique N. Walker, Ed.D. has to share! If you want more in-depth reflections, stay tuned for additional learning opportunities including a companion workbook, webinars, and workshops. More resources and strategies will be provided, which are designed to help you on your leadership journey and provide additional support to help you grapple with each of the insights outlined in this book. Visit www.vnwconsulting.com for information about upcoming publications and events.

Acknowledgments

While reading my personal journals for *Underestimated*, I realized that the desire to encourage others by writing a book about my experiences budded in my mid-twenties, which was approximately 20 years ago. With this in mind, I am elated to see my dream fulfilled by completing my first book, the process of which was supported by key people to whom I extend a heartfelt thanks.

My Mother—who was and is my ultimate example of perseverance—regularly inquired about the status of my book, which kept me writing. She asked insightful questions after reading an initial draft that helped me clarify important details.

Bray, who *consistently* encouraged me to put "wings on the book," was a sounding board and also helped with designing the cover, crafting content, and providing guidance for key elements. His encouragement was priceless in completing the book.

Vernetta who served as a reader and provided feedback on the relatability of the content, particularly in areas of spirituality. She has been a source of inspiration for many years, and I appreciate her continual positive and peaceful presence.

Sammie who also served as a reader and helped me focus on writing more concisely. Her words helped me to review the content for impact versus details.

Dorothy who was a positive source of energy and connected me to essential resources as the project was nearing completion.

Tara and Nicole whose enthusiasm about the project propelled me forward.

There are many others, by virtue of being family or friends, who have been an inspiration to me as well—including Craig, Lisa, Devin, Wendy, Brenden, Bryant, Leia, Brasen, and Beverly H.

Last, my story could not be told without discussing the central source of my strength, which is God the Father, God the Son (Jesus), and God the Holy Spirit. . .to whom I give the greatest thanks!

About the Author

Dr. Veronique N. Walker has over 22 years of experience serving in the field of education and the helping profession. Dr. Walker is a 1995 graduate of Shepherd University where she earned a Bachelor of Arts degree in psychology. She has earned a Master of Arts degree in counseling from Marshall University, and a Doctor of Education degree in organizational leadership and certification in administration and supervision from Shenandoah University. Additionally, Dr. Walker is a licensed professional counselor, a national certified counselor, and holds various other certifications.

Dr. Walker enjoys spending time with family and friends, music, writing, and traveling. She values the trait of perseverance—for she has experienced that perseverance is the essence of any desired goal. Because of her experiences, one her goals is to empower others to disrupt the limitations that life experiences, self, and others may have used to hinder them.

Appendix A
Recommended Resources

CliftonStrengths Online Talent Assessment
Identifies a person's top talents and strengths.
Cost: different prices based on individual, team, organization, or student.
https://www.gallup.com/cliftonstrengths/en/252137/home.aspx

Disc & Spiritual Profile – ARC Churches
Assists individuals in identifying and developing their leadership style.
Cost: Free
https://www.arcchurches.com/disc/

High 5 Test
Designed to identify a person's natural abilities.
Cost: Free or a fee for more in-depth assessment.
https://high5test.com/

Myers-Briggs Type Indicator® (MBTI®) Personality Assessment
Provides insight about your personality.
Cost: $49.95
https://www.mbtionline.com

Project Implicit – Harvard University

Measures a person's attitudes and beliefs about different cultural and societal factors.

Cost: Free

https://implicit.harvard.edu/implicit/

Notes

[1] Underestimate. (n.d.). In *Oxford Learner's Dictionaries.* Retrieved on June 24, 2020, from https://www.oxfordlearnersdictionaries.com/us/definition/english/underestimate_1?q=underestimate

[2] Jer. 29:11 (NLT). "For I know the plans I have for you," says the Lord. "They are plans for good and not for disaster, to give you a future and a hope."

[3] Day, D. V., & Antonakis, J. (2012). Leadership: Past, present, and future. In D. V. Day, & J. Antonakis (Eds.), *The Nature of Leadership, Second Edition* (pp. 3-25). Thousand Oaks, CA: Sage Publications, Inc.

[4] Wooi, C. T., Salleh, L. M., & Ismail, I. A. (2017). Lessons from the major leadership theories in comparison to the competency theory for leadership practice. *Journal of Business and Social Review in Emerging Economies, 3*(2), 147-156. Retrieved from https://publishing.globalcsrc.org/ojs/index.php/jbsee/article/view/86

[5] Day and Antonakis, Leadership, pp. 3-25.

6 Johnson, A. M., Vernon, P. A., McCarthy, J. M., Molson, M., Harris, J. A., & Jang, K. L. (1998, August). Nature vs. nurture: Are leaders born or made? A genetic investigation of leadership style. *Twin Research and Genetic Studies, 1*(4), 216-223. DOI: https://doi.org/10.1375/twin.1.4.216

7 Prov. 27:19 (NLT). "As a face is reflected in water, so the heart reflects the real person."

8 Ps. 1:6 (NLT). "For the LORD watches over the path of the godly, but the path of the wicked leads to destruction."

9 Sanchez-Hucles, J. V., & Davis, D. D. (2010). Women and women of color in leadership: Complexity, identity, and intersectionality. *American Psychologist, 65*(3), 171–181. Retrieved from DOI: 10.1037/a0017459

10 Microaggression. (n.d.). In *Merriam-Webster.com Dictionary.* Retrieved September 19, 2020, from https://www.merriamwebster.com/dictionary/microaggression

11 Walker, V. N. (2014). African American women superintendents: Perceptions of barriers and strategies accessing the superintendency (Doctoral dissertation). Retrieved from ProQuest Dissertations and Full Theses. (UMI No. 3582087)

12 Prov. 24:16a (NLT). "The godly may trip seven times, but they will get up again."

[13] Jackson, B. L. (1999). Getting inside history-against all odds: African American women school superintendents. In C. C. Brunner, (Ed.), *Sacred dreams: Women and the superintendency* (pp. 141-159). Albany, NY: State University of New York Press.

[14] Ps. 94:19 (NIV). "When anxiety was great within me, your consolation brought me joy."

[15] Gal. 6:9 (NIV). "Let us not become weary in doing good, for at the proper time we will reap a harvest if we do not give up."

[16] Zech. 4:10a (NKJV). "For who has despised the day of small things?"

[17] Culture shock. In *Merriam-Webster.com Dictionary*. Retrieved June 19, 2019, from https://www.merriam-webster.com/dictionary/culture%20shock

[18] Combs, J. P., Edmonson, S., & Harris, S. (2013). *The trust factor: Strategies for school leaders*. New York: Routledge.

[19] Luke 6:38 (NLT). "Give, and you will receive. Your gift will return to you in full—pressed down, shaken together to make room for more, running over, and poured into your lap. The amount you give will determine the amount you get back."

[20] Rom. 5:3-4 (NIV). "[3] Not only so, but we[a] also glory in our sufferings, because we know that suffering produces perseverance; [4] perseverance, character; and character, hope."

[21] Phil. 4:8 (NLT). "And now, dear brothers and sisters, one final thing. Fix your thoughts on what is true, and honorable, and right, and pure, and lovely, and admirable. Think about things that are excellent and worthy of praise."

[22] Ferris, G. R., Harris, J. N., Russell, Z. A., & Maher, L. P. (2018). Politics in organizations. In D. S. Ones, N. Anderson, C. Viswesvaran, & H. K. Sinangil (Eds.), The SAGE handbook of industrial, work & organizational psychology: Organizational psychology (p. 469–486). Sage Reference.

[23] Buchanan, D. A., & Badham, R. J. (2008). *Power, politics, and organizational change: Winning the turf game.* (2nd ed.) Los Angeles; London: SAGE Publications. Retrieved from https://pdfs.semanticscholar.org/bc50/4704c5f93317f13c1656287ce24df59107ce.pdf

[24] Hill, C., Miller, K., Benson, K., & Handley, G. (2016). Barriers and bias: The status of women in leadership. Washington, DC: American Association of University Women. Retrieved from https://www.aauw.org/resources/research/barrier-bias/

[25] Goryunova, E., Scribner, R. T., & Madsen, S. R. (2017). The current status of women leaders worldwide. In S. R. Madsen, *Handbook of Research on Gender and Leadership* (pp. 3-23). Northampton, Massachusetts, USA: Edward Elgar Publishing, Inc. Retrieved from https://www.elgaronline.com/view/edcoll/9781785363856/9781785363856.00008.xml

Made in the USA
Middletown, DE
06 November 2020